Jonah and the Whale

Jonah and the Whale

words by Jessica d'Este
illustrations Ian Pentney

IMPRESS

Long before now
But after the beginning
In God's city of Nineveh
God's people were sinning

As has happened before
And may happen again
A people gone mad
Being wicked and bad
Making God angry
Making God sad.

The question arises
What to do when
This happens to prevent it
Happening again.

God's reply was to send
His Prophet Jonah at speed
To warn his people of grief
The riposte of their greed.

But Jonah was wayward –
As far as could be
From doing God's will –
He ran off, went to sea.

Whereupon, a great storm
A rout and rumbling of waves
Made all aboard tremble
Made the sailors afraid

Sensing God's anger
All aboard prayed.

And the lot fell to Jonah
To jump ship for you see
The sailors thought: Aha! Jonah!
They suspected 'twas he
Raised the temper of God
And the tempest at sea.

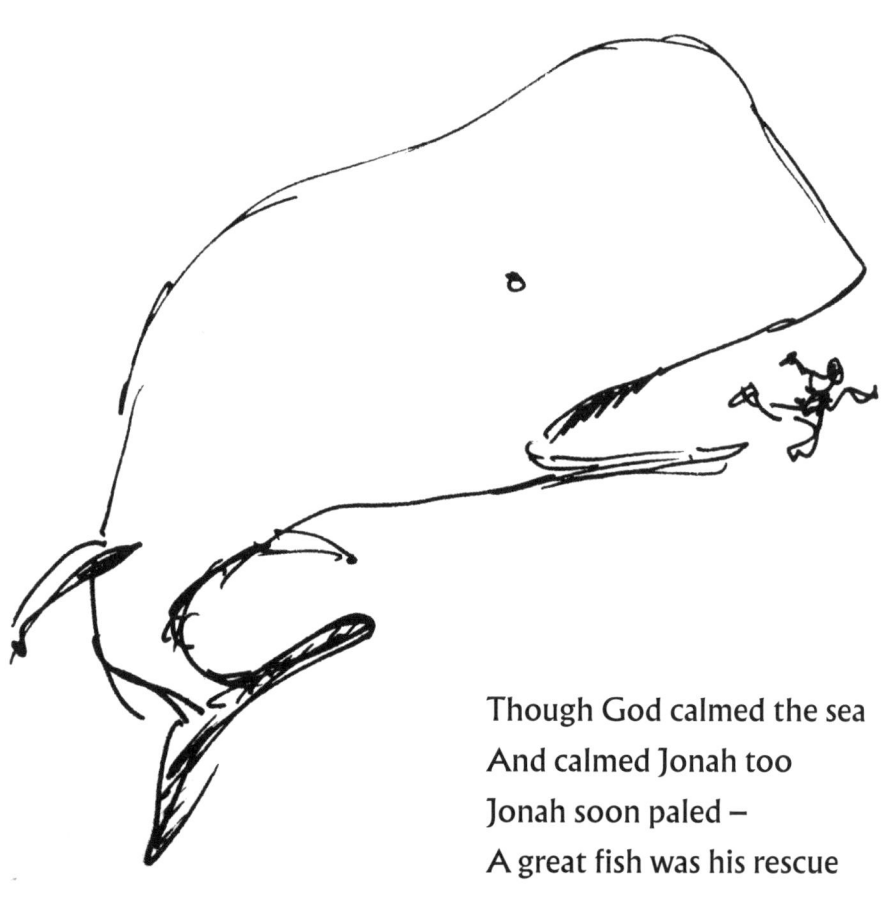

Though God calmed the sea
And calmed Jonah too
Jonah soon paled –
A great fish was his rescue

With a whale of a grin
That landed him in
A whale of a belly –
'Twas God's will to save him.

Three days and three nights so
'Til the fish spat him out
And God, again, ordered: Go!
Commanding Jonah to shout:

No more! Enough Nineveh!
For God's sake, rescind!
Forty days more
And God's patience will end.

Nineveh's people
Bad but nor daft
Listened to Jonah
Tempered God's wrath

So beloved again
And no longer bad
They basked in God's mercy
Forgiven and glad.

Jonah, however
As sullen a priest
As e'er left a city
As e'er travelled East

Resented God's wisdom
Sat apart though he knew
He needed God's help
To know what to do.

So God sent a sign
As so often of old
And that sign is the reason
This story is told:

God made an oil plant
Live and die in one day
Jonah's shelter in ruins!
But its demise was God's way

Of showing Jonah and all us
His will from above
Is long life for his people
In return for their love.

Limited edtion of 100 copies
signed by the poet and
the illustrator

number 71/100

Published in 2018 by Impress

Impress
Editorial Department [156]
95 Wilton Road
London, sw1v 1bz

ISBN 978 0 9955540 8 5
www.impress-publishing.com

Designed by Prof. Phil Cleaver
and George Gallagher
of et al design consultants.
Typeset in Monotype Albertus Nova
Print production by Dave Davies
of DLM Creative.
Printed in England by Hartgraph.